MY DADDY ALWAYS SAID

Copyright © 2019 C. Birdfinger

All Rights Reserved.

ISBN: 978-1-7331452-7-5

Dedicated to
the Daddy's who have more than nothing
and less than everything
and to
the Momma's who helped
their babies grow up
to be or not to be.

WARNING
STAY BACK TWO HUNDRED MILES
NOT RESPONSIBLE FOR

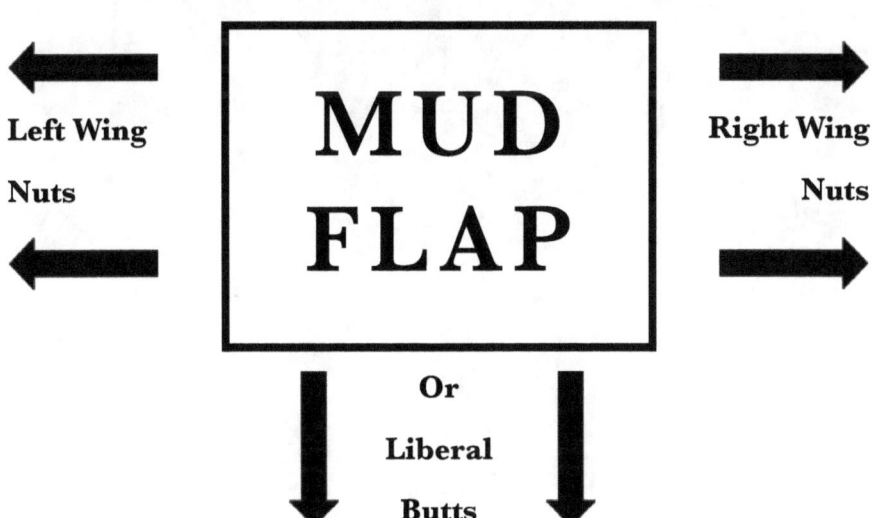

Sardines, Beans, Himoroids, Heroroids, and Things **My Daddy Always Said**

My daddy always said there were seven times seventy Democrats at the altar of undone. They were all scheming on how to unseat the elected chosen one. They had tried every lie, every trick, looking for a way to have another Dick to kick around; until the silent majority's feet hit the ground. When the smoke clears, and the traitors are brought to trial, this time it will be the conservatives who get to smile.

My daddy always said when the Bureau of Land Management offered one thousand dollars to anyone who would adopt a horse but only fifty dollars to adopt an ass, not one single Democrat was adopted.

My daddy always said Trump is great, Trump is good – let us thank him for kicking the Democrats asses good. So... Mr. President, kick-em while they're up, kick-em when they're down. Kick their asses all over D.C. 'crat' town.

My daddy always said when Nancy Pelosi told the Democratic members of congress that they needed to stop the leaks or Trump would know all their plans, the men bought vag-a-seal and the women bought fix-a-flat.

My daddy always said if after all the books that were bought for you, and all the teachers that taught you... if you still don't know a damn thing – there's always politics.

My daddy always said Bill Clinton's epitaph should read: "I got it in the kitchen, I got it in the hall, I got it in the oval office so screw you all."

My daddy always said he always believed the hell hole was located below Hillary Clinton's nose until Trump pointed out it was in Baltimore Maryland.

My daddy always said never marry a woman whose ass is the neighborhoods gravy train.

My daddy always said, what did the hooker say to the john after a choke and poke? 'I hope your wife likes crabs!'

My daddy always said when Nancy Pelosi was stopped by T.S.A. before boarding her plane because she was leading Alexandria Ocasio Cortez on a short leash, she explained, 'This is my support animal.'

My daddy always said when the judge asked Patriots owner, Robert Kraft, just what the hell he was thinking – Kraft replied, "Your honor, the Chinese are famous for their pulled pork and my poker needed a good pulling."

My daddy always said it's not the monsters under your bed, it's the monsters in somebody's head you have to worry about.

My daddy always said that Nancy Pelosi and Chuck Schumer are so close that every time Nancy takes a douche, Chuck takes a shower.

My daddy always said what did the doctor say to the Speaker of the House about her hemorrhoid? "Nancy, I've seen fire and Nancy, I've seen rain but Nancy, I can't understand why you let A.O.C. cause you so much pain."

My daddy always said wonder what song the patriot's owner was singing in his head when he was at the Chinese massage parlor in Florida? "When the – "Saints" - Go Marching In or My Heroes Have Always Been the – "Cowboys?"

My daddy always said when House Speaker Nancy Pelosi was caught sneaking out of Alexandria Ocasio Cortez's office the reporter asked what she was doing to which the speaker replied, 'I just dropped in to see what condition my condition was in.'

My daddy always said when Jack Nicholson moved to Los Angeles to become an actor, he named his penis 'the truth.' That's why he was so convincing in the movie when he snarled at Tom Cruise those famous words, "You can't handle the truth."

My daddy always said wave to the Democrats with your left-hand, wave to the Republicans with your right hand but salute the liberals with your Birdfinger.

My Daddy Always Said

My daddy always said what happened when ro – bot Muller testified before congress on Trumps investigation? Mueller put his hands over his eyes; next he put his hands over his ears; then he put his hands over his mouth. He just wanted to remind Americans he saw no evil – he heard no evil – so he spoke no evil.

My daddy always said ladies and gentlemen, dogs and cats, bow-legged mosquitoes and baldheaded Democrats. Elijah Cummings has a monopoly on rodents and rats. While Tulsi Gabbard has a monopoly on, "Kitty, kitty, kitty, here kitty, kitty, I'm your huckleberry."

My daddy always said when Senator Elizabeth Warren didn't know the answer to how many feet there are in a foot, everyone knew she was a fake-a-hontas.

My daddy always said somebody should tell the U.S. Fish and Wildlife that there are several senators and congresswomen walking around with dead beavers.

My daddy always said what did Arkansas Bill say to his pig in a poke on their wedding night? "Let's play squeal or no squeal?"

My daddy always said since Florida is known as the penis of the United States does that make Georgia, Alabama, Mississippi, and Louisiana the balls of the United States? If so – that would make "big ole goodins" and "good ole biggins" never a bad one "tex" the "ass" of the United States.

My daddy always said doctors have discovered the best age to stop breast-feeding millennials - after 30 years, snowflakes after 35 years, gamers after 16 years, geezers and lesbians - till death do them 'breast' part.

My daddy always said since Pete Buttigieg can't use the pronoun to describe his ass anymore, what description will he use; manhole or maintenance hole?

My daddy always said what do you call a beaver with a vagina? Duh – a beaver.

My daddy always said if you Democrats can't smell my ass that means soap and water works. Go ahead, give it a try. I dare you!

My daddy always said if it waddles like a duck, quacks like a duck, it must be none other than Congress – 'mun' Jerry Nadler from 'nu – yoke – tate.'

My daddy always said when his first girlfriend named her ass satisfaction and kicked him to the curb, all he could do for months was sing, "I can't get no satisfaction."

My daddy always said God gave you a mouth. God gave you a brain. God gave you sense enough to get in out of the rain. So, if you stand on your head and piss on your dreams, don't cry oh God, and blame him for anything.

My daddy always said you can't fix stupid – but you sure as hell can elect stupid – 'right Nancy?'

My daddy always said since you can't say ladies and gentlemen anymore, can you at least say hooters and cooters?

My daddy always said what did the lesbian say to the protester who wanted her to join the march on less meat – less heat - climate change? "Look honey, I've been getting less meat all my life. Go peddle that crap to the wives and hookers."

My Daddy always said it is what it is, it ain't what it ain't. Some people will still touch it, to see if it's wet paint.

My daddy always said when the judge asked Patriots owner Robert Kraft what he had to say for himself – Kraft replied, "I like Chinese."

My daddy always said when you figure out how many feet there are in a foot then you are ready to become a politician.

My daddy always said if you have never seen a doofus then you've never been to a D. M. V. counter.

My daddy always said the only difference between tree rats and dem-rats is one plays in trees and the other plays with Republicans.

My daddy always said if there is no place like home then why the hell are you taking a vacation?

My daddy always said if you can have a Dr. Ho on TV selling something you pump, why can't you have a street ho on TV selling something you hump?

My daddy always said if you keep seeing skid marks in your underwear it's time for you to take ass-wiping lessons.

My daddy always said when Democrats die, they are reincarnated into hemorrhoids on a Republican's ass.

My daddy always said when it comes down to thoughts and prayers "thoughts are for the perverts and prayers are for the converts."

My daddy always said the Nan-chu's of the Democrats are starting to give out Indian names to their members. Alexandria Ocasio Cortez will be known as "Kitty Two Bits." Beto O'Rourke will be known as "Talking Turd Eater." Elizabeth "Hontas" Warren will be known as "Monkey Spanker."

My daddy always said since the Kentucky Governor, Matt Bevin signed a bill into law which outlaws' sex between humans and animals, does that mean Republicans and Democrats can no longer have sex in Kentucky?

My daddy always said while driving down a country road he saw a sign in a field that read, "When this grass is baled, it will come out of the field as hay."

My daddy always said mommas don't let your babies grow up to be Democrats. They will lie, cheat, steal, and grow up to act like Nancy, Chuck, and Bill.

My daddy always said ever since Tail-U-Ride started using Oprah's ass as a downhill ski jump, things have become stanky.

My daddy always said when the Patriots Big Cheese came before the judge and said your honor, there were ten fingers moving faster than light and I wanted it to last all night but Trumps Chinese tariffs were about to start and I was about to fart, so the only thing I could do was start singing… hold on, I'm coming – hold on, I'm coming.

My daddy always said when Chick-fil-A lost the highest bid to filet Jennifer Garner's dead chicken, all the vegans said 8men and were sued by the alphabet for not saying 4-men and 4 women.

My daddy always said Democrat councilman Gross wants to decriminalize sex work in the District of Columbia so all the Democrat politicians can be out of jail at the same time.

My daddy always said if Running Bear had married "a politician called Naked" she would have been known as "Running Bear Naked".

My daddy always said when your ass is as big as Texas, that's called tex − ass.

My daddy always said if Pink married George Bush, would she be known as George's Pink Bush or Ms. Pink Bush?

My daddy always said the big difference between a Democrat 'cat' and a Republican 'cat' is a Republican 'cat' will get up off it's ass, catch, kill and eat a rat. A Democrat 'cat' will lay on its lazy ass and wait for the Republicans to feed it.

My daddy always said the only difference between a pig and a poke is one will give you bacon, the other can give you an S.T.D.

My daddy always said the only difference between snakes and politicians is there are some good snakes.

My daddy always said marry a woman with a butter face. I asked, "Daddy, what is a butter face? Son, it's where everything about her looks good but-her face."

My daddy always said when Whoopi farts under the tents she wears, is it classified gale force or tail force winds?

My daddy always said since 60% of people never wash their hands after using the restroom and 40% only rinse, this means if you shake their hand, you might as well be kissing their ass.

My daddy always said - if a dog has no knees and a mosquito has no fleas but a monkey has a tail and a hamburger won't keep you out of jail - then why believe in magic?

My daddy always said when your ass makes a deposit your brain can't cash, don't expect taxpayers to pay for your stitches.

My daddy always said some idiots live long enough to get their driver's license and become idiots driving.

My daddy always said if you got flies following you around, it's either time to crawl back in the grave or take a bath.

My daddy always said when it comes to picking your nose or scratching your ass, everybody is ambidextrous.

My daddy always said just because you can write does not mean you are always right. All it means is you are a Democrat who got past third grade.

My daddy always said the mouth is the front door, the ass is the back door so don't speak anything out the front door that will get the back door kicked in.

My daddy always said Christopher Columbus discovered America, even though people were already living here. Al Gore discovered the Internet, even though people were already using it and Hillary Clinton discovered there are 50 states not 13 colonies.

My daddy always said if Snoop Dogg married Martha Stewart he would forever be known as Martha's dog.

My daddy always said if Maxine Waters married Vladimir Putin and opened an Inn in Smells, Texas she would be known as Maxine Waters Putin Smells Inn Texas.

My daddy always said if balls are called go-nads shouldn't breasts be called naw-nads?

My daddy always said there are two things to never add to your bucket list "french kiss an alligator" and "wipe the ass of a rattlesnake".

My daddy always said when you start hearing voices make sure they're not telling you that you are short, fat, and squatty - all ass - and - no - body.

My daddy always said his first date must have wiped her mouth with her ass because her breath smelled like shit.

My daddy always said the cows have been calling some woe-mans on The View wanting their moo-moo's back.

My daddy always said if you go to bed with a Chupacabra don't expect to wake up with a fox.

My daddy always said the only difference between a politician and a thief is one robs you with a gun, the other robs you with a promise.

My daddy always said the only difference between a politician and a plate of beans is one blows hot air up your ass and the other blows hot air out your ass.

My daddy always said if you have the hook – line and sinker, there is always a fish out there dumb enough to bite.

My daddy always said there is absolutely no difference between a politician and a polecat because both, given the chance will put the stink on you.

My daddy always said a camel toe will never fit through the eye of a needle.

My daddy always said Hillary was the luckiest blind squirrel known to mankind. She found millions of nuts to vote for her.

My daddy always said Trump's state of the union address should have been, "Come one, come all ye Democrats crawl up my legs where you can all have a ball."

My daddy always said some of the definitions of a politician are "shrewd, crafty, unscrupulous and polyp." So, every election cycle when you feel that pressure up your rectum, "that's not smoke Toto, that politicians.

My daddy always said the doctors in India were unsuccessful in removing a 250-pound himorrhoid from Hillary Clinton's ass; Trump just wouldn't let go.

My daddy always said to my mama, "You say you love me, you say you need me, can't live without me... so why do you run out of the room every time I cut the cheese?"

My daddy always said what do you get when you subtract a liberal from a Democrat? Nothing – 'absolutely nothing' say it again – nothing – 'absolutely nothing.'

My daddy always said the woe-mans of The View and Oprah are suing Trump because when they were downtown – uptown – around town - just looking for some touch, Trump wouldn't even walk their way.

My daddy always said when the judge asked Patriots owner Robert Kraft to explain his actions he said, 'Your honor, I was looking for a thrill so I took a little blue pill – then I couldn't chill so I went to a Chinese fire drill because all the Russians were under investigation.'

My daddy always said there are pitchers and catchers. Trump was a pitcher – Hillary was a catcher and when Hillary got up to bat, Trump struck her out.

My daddy always said politicians and flies – politicians and flies the more I see of politicians the more I like flies.

My daddy always said when John Smith looked out over the fort walls and saw an Indian maiden doing cartwheels with no underwear on, it wasn't long before he was poking – hontas.

My daddy always said when it's a hundred degrees outside and you are riding an elevator with someone who has the farts, what will you be wearing all day? "Their stanky fart smell."

My daddy always said when you have someone's foot up your ass – go directly to I'm sorry, leave you 'son of a bitch' in Al Gore's lockbox.

My daddy always said friends are just like the weather – they're totally unpredictable.

My daddy always said when the brain is constipated, and the mouth has diarrhea you are opening the door to an ass whipping.

My daddy always said the doctors that discovered a cure for "foot in mouth," disease, wondered why it failed to cure politicians.

My daddy always said the Mississippi Delta farmers are in a row – versus - wade situation. They have to wade out into their fields to see if they still have a row to plant or row to hoe.

My daddy always said when he was shopping in Saks on Fifth Avenue in New York City, he saw a couple that was a perfect ten. The 'she' was a '1' and 'he' was a '0' on the scale, making them a perfect '10'.

My daddy always said Nancy Pee Loosely is holding prayer vigils for Alexandria Ocasio Cortez. They're praying no one lets the air out of her head before she can be sworn in as a Congresswoman for New York State.

My daddy always said if life had given him roses instead of rattlesnakes, winners instead of losers, hemorrhoids instead of herorhoids, he wouldn't have to be pissing in the wind just to take a shower.

My daddy always said a furniture store in Houston, Texas has the best advertisement ever. "Buy your furniture from me and get your ass spanked for free!"

My daddy always said if it's illegal for airplanes to fly over the White House, why shouldn't it be illegal for President Trump to let air heads in the White House?

My daddy always said the big difference between jam and jelly is no one ever called you up and said, 'I'm in a jelly, can you help me out?'

My daddy always said if you get rear ended grab the Preparation H with pain relief, not the phone. If you call that lawyer all you'll get is de-bone.

My daddy always said when he was little he could toot and poot with the best of ease. Now that he is old and gray, any squeeze and a turd his ass could lay.

My daddy always said when Hillary was asked how long she wanted to lie in state she replied, "I've lied in every damn state at least a dozen times. That should be enough to keep the hell fires burning."

My daddy always said when Richard Nixon resigned, he said, "You won't have my dick to kick around anymore."

My daddy always said Nancy Pelosi is no longer Speaker of the House since A.O.C. and Omar took over. She is now known as weaker of the house.

My daddy always said if you are crazy enough to jump off a cliff - jump off naked. That way on your way down you can kiss your own crazy ass goodbye.

My daddy always said all the V– Gina hat marchers are pondering a class action lawsuit because Trump wouldn't touch their V– Gina's even with Anthony's Weiner.

My daddy always said most of us don't like it, but fast food workers are going to pop their zits.

My daddy always said you will never find anyone having a titty party having a pity party.

My daddy always said life is an asshole and we are all just passing through it. Death is like a buzzard buffet where relatives are looking for any sign of meat on a bone, "that's called a will."

My daddy always said somebody should tell Serena Williams that there's a walker tennis tournament. It's the one where you can put tennis balls on your walker to move faster.

My daddy always said since the Clearwater police and the Naples Daily News made sure everyone knew the alligator that broke into a local home was a male, he wondered why didn't they bother to ask that male gator if he wanted to go by a Chinese massage parlor and get his Robert Kraft on.

My daddy always said when will the Republicans wake up from their fear naps and start eating common sense with a helping of use it or lose it?

My daddy always said when everything fails, call a Republican. When everything goes right, call a Democrat and thank them for letting the Republicans fix the problems.

My daddy always said when the day comes that the left is right, it's time to worry and lose sleep at night.

My daddy always said if the "pee" is yellow let it mellow. If "it" is brown, flush it down. If "it" is green name it A.O.C.

My daddy always said there is a new book about to hit the bookstores. It's title, "Why Do" says it all. Why do men go fishing when they complain about women that smell like fish? Why do women prune – pick – paint and pucker just to reel in a 'sucker' – 'not a fish'? A sucker of life, who will suck all the ambition, hopes, dreams, pride, self-esteem, confidence and all that 'can do attitude' right out of their pretty little heads.

My daddy always said that Whoopi was lying on the floor in a fetal position crying, "Where are my reparations," when Joy said, "The dingoes ate your reparations."

My daddy always said just because a fly flies into your mouth doesn't mean it's time to eat.

My daddy always said when your beloved has one foot out the door, don't just stand there. Help them get that other foot out, before they change their mind.

My daddy always said if you are a writer, write. If you are a singer, sing. If you are an actor, act, but if you are politician - quit lying.

My daddy always said what did Congressman Elijah Cummings say to the people of his Maryland District when they asked him to care and do for them as much as he pretended to care and do for the illegal aliens at the border? "Shut up! It's not election time, I'll hear you when I need your vote."

My daddy always said since politicians have voted in medically assisted suicide, they should have to be the first ones to try it out to see if it works.

My daddy always said if you are bowlegged from riding the horse of failure then get off, stand up straight, and join the Republican party.

My daddy always said a three-ring circus is when an election comes to town. The politicians are the clowns because you never know who they are until they take their make-up off.

My daddy always said political men parade their wife and kids around at election time, to try to prove they are macho men, then when they're elected, they go back to wearing tutus and yoga pants.

My daddy always said the only difference between cow poo and a cow patty is where you step.

My daddy always said before you make another excuse, check to see how far your wife's foot is up your ass.

My daddy always said if you wake up with a lizard in your hair you've been somewhere you shouldn't have been, or your friendly lizard is just enjoying a lice breakfast.

My daddy always said if you can't see the light at the end of the tunnel then get your head out of your ass.

My daddy always said Sue was riding Johnny's back when she slipped and slid down past his butt crack. The smell was so bad she lost her breath and that was written in stone as cause of death.

My daddy always said he had seen possums, he had seen pigs, he had eaten cherries, he had eaten figs, he had tasted raindrops from the sky, he had cursed at a horsefly, he had jumped high, he had jumped low, he had run fast, he had run slow, but he had never met an honest politician.

My daddy always said you don't have to lay down with dogs to get fleas. If you play your cards wrong, your other half will start bringing them home.

My daddy always said opinions are like farts in the wind. They come out stinking to high heaven and solve nothing.

My daddy always said when he heard that charity begins at home, he changed my sister's name.

My daddy always said when you think you know it all, look in the mirror and you will see a fool.

My daddy always said the short will always be short. The tall will always be tall, but the important things in life can't be measured at all.

My daddy always said the only guarantee in life is death and the only guarantee in death, wait, there are no guarantees in death… because you're just dead.

My daddy always said if you have the bull by the horns then let go and grab life by the hair of its chinny-chin-chin and hang on for the ride of your life.

My daddy always said when you're just killing time, you are only robbing yourself.

My daddy always said when fake-a-hontas Warren went to the doctor for a check-up, the doctor asked if she had been using Round-Up – to which she replied, "No, but if it will help my sagging ass, I'll start using it."

My daddy always said when showering after someone, make sure to wash their ass off the soap before washing your face.

My daddy always said if you are full of sardines, beer and beans don't go knocking on her door.

My daddy always said the difference between a male man and a mail-man is one has a pair and the other delivers cards from Democrats begging for money.

My daddy always said, 'if I ever get the money, I'm going to sue Marie Osmond because that 50 pounds she lost, your mother found it.'

My daddy always said it was raining- it was hot- everybody was happy - no one was not - laughter was passed around like mashed potatoes and gravy - things were growing, bellies were full - then the politicians came on stage.

My daddy always said you find rats in Democrats and cans in Republicans. You get to decide which one you want to be.

My daddy always said — what do you hear? Rats cumming, - what do you see? Rodents cumming, - where do you hear them cumming — 'Baltimore," — where do you see them cumming — "Baltimore." What does the congressmun say now, that the world knows he is the landlord of Maryland's hellhole?

My daddy always said a baby is like a tomato. First you have a seed - then a plant - then a blossom - then a green tomato. If you protect it from bugs - worms - and other blue insects, water and fertilize it, you will have a red ripe conservative, and everyone will ahh with admiration that it is a Republican.

My daddy always said Trump was pissed off when Billy got the Bush and all he got was a Hillary up the ass.

My daddy always said the best beat down award goes to Tulsi Gabbard for spanking Kamala Harris with her own sadistic record while she was Attorney General of California. 'Stand by for thong wars."

My daddy always said when Julia Roberts took her yearly bath and Sheryl Crow used her yearly supply of two squares of toilet paper at the same time the world said no-men.

My daddy always said the halls of justice were designed for and supported by the "politicians and the privileged for only the politicians are the privileged."

My daddy always said somebody somewhere is taking their last breath, somebody somewhere is taking their first breath, somebody somewhere is farting their last fart, and somebody somewhere is farting their first fart. Which one are you?

My daddy always said when you are drunk on ignorance and staggering on starvation don't come knock – knock – knocking on heaven's door, for she is in bed with "I want more out of life."

My daddy always said when the doctor is pushing on your hemorrhoids and both his hands are on your shoulders, you should have sense enough to know something is rotten in Denmark and it's not the cheese.

My daddy always said never measure someone's ass with an axe handle when you need a yard stick.

My daddy always said there are three women who will never be walking around with a perky Brazilian butt and Oprah is all four of them.

My daddy always said Senator Dianne Feinstein is wanting to trade off a used Ford that's been ugly tested, that's a liar, that went pass go, that collected millions of dollars and laughed all the way to the bank.

My daddy always said the Democrats have a century old law. All Republicans in both houses of congress must surrender their balls and back bone before being sworn in.

My daddy always said when the demon-crats held another 'de – bait' on July thirtieth, twenty nineteen, they picked the right month because they were all singing Ju – lie, Ju – lie, u – lie, we all lie in Ju – ly.

My daddy always said never trust a man with sideburns or a woman with rugburns.

My daddy always said girls and squirrels are just alike; they both love nuts.

My daddy always said, 'put your finger in, dig around, pull your finger out, sling it on the ground… that's how you go booger hunting.'

My daddy always said don't ever try to count the stars when you have hung the moon.

My daddy always said the difference between a her and a him is with her you can get a him but with him you're liable to get anything.

My daddy always said what did C.N.N. learn about parading the presidential hopefuls across the Ju – lie stage in Detroit City on 7-30-19? Not one single two brain cell American swallowed de - bait.

My daddy always said Maryland had a little Elijah who had fleeced the people of Baltimore of all their votes while promising to send them Mexicans with goats to do all the work that makes their boats float. Trump pulled the curtain back and exposed to the world that what Baltimore has is rodents with demo-rats and a boss rat.

My daddy always said the only difference between shingles and shingles is one covers the house from rain, the other one covers your ass with pain.

My daddy always said when your ass is dragging the ground, it's time to start exercising.

My daddy always said when you wet your wick in a witch don't act surprised when they turn into a Democrat.

My daddy always said if Rosie O'Donnell married The Jolly Green Giant then divorced and married Anthony Weiner she would then be known as Rosie's Giant Weiner.

My daddy always said mankind would be better served if politicians had to bend over and let the sunshine in.

My daddy always said since some states want live birth abortion why can't they have snowflake abortion, up to say… age twenty-six.

My daddy always said butts and bridges are alike, both can handle heavy traffic.

My daddy always said the big difference between a condor and a canary is the size of their turds.

My daddy always said when your spirit guide gets drunk and wrecks your life, it's time to trade that sucker in for a new one.

My daddy always said the only difference between Putin and pootin is one comes out the ass as a fart the other rules Russia without a heart.

C. Birdfinger

My daddy always said that Kildee legs, - Martin thighs, great big head and baboon eyes only describes half of all actors. The other half is not worthy of a description.

My daddy always said if you drink and eat from the table and fountain of ignorance, you will surely become a fool.

My daddy always said you can easily tell the difference between an old goat and a goat. The old goat has two legs the other is a Democrat.

My daddy always said if you pick your nose in bed then you'll have boogers under the covers.

My daddy always said it is far better to kill a million ants than one monkey's uncle.

My daddy always said Santa Claus has spent his whole life trying to trade his presents for some ho-ho- ho's.

My daddy always said a politician begs and gets forgiveness for cheating again and again. A preacher gets forgiveness for their cheating sin but the average Joe - people will never forget or let go when he is caught sleeping with a ho.

My daddy always said the difference between mowing and ho-ing is one is cutting grass, the other is spreading ass.

My daddy always said Elijah Cummings is missing the perfect chance to become a superhero. All he needs to do is bring in some North Koreans – set them up in the restaurants all over the city of Baltimore – let them do the work Americans won't do. They will catch and cook all the rats and feed them to all the elected Washington, D.C. fat cats. The snowflakes will buy him a cape and he will be known as the super 'rat' man. Now, who could be his super 'rat' woman, Nancy?

My daddy always said friends are a dime a dozen; as-long-as you have a dime you can buy a dozen.

My daddy always said if you come to a fork in the road, pick it up and start eating the crow in your life.

My daddy always said Hillary was pissed beyond repair when she found out Bill had got it in the kitchen – got it in the hall but got it in the oval office most of all.

My daddy always said the best way to stop your boss from chewing your ass out is to start using preparation work.

My daddy always said actors, singers and politicians proudly show off their pre-K IQ when they talk without a script.

My daddy always said caffeine and hemorrhoids paddle the same boat. One wakes up the brain the other keeps the ass awake.

My daddy always said if you "plan to fail" vote Democrat - if you "fail to plan" vote liberal - if you have "no plan at all," vote Republican.

My daddy always said when you know it all - all you know is nothing.

My daddy always said vows that bind can be separated with time and wine.

My daddy always said presidential hopeful Kirsten Gillibrand, Senator from New York, has the bright idea (her only idea) to hire Hillary Clinton's staff to 'bleach bit' clean the oval office where slick Willie came face to face with Monica Lewinsky.

My daddy always said when Santa Claus was arrested for trying to breed Beanie Weenie with Beanie Babies to get "Pokem Hot Hyenas" his defense "In – Santa -ty."

My daddy always said the big difference between Pee and Pea is one comes out water and the other comes out poo.

My daddy always said your as-s good as-s gold twice as shiny "butt that is" not a good excuse for a stinking hinny, Julia.

My daddy always said if your significant other has warts on their ass and warts on their nose it still doesn't make them a warthog.

My daddy always said have you been exposed to ass-worst-us? If you have been in a crowd, an elevator or a port-a-potty and the smell is so bad you wear it home, then you have been exposed to ass-worst-us. Make that one call – get your thirty-nine cents on.

My daddy always said when you keep repeating "you know what I'm saying" even you are too stupid to know what you're saying.

My daddy always said the cure for foot and mouth disease is keep your mouth shut and people will keep their foot out of your ass.

My daddy always said was that just old Joe massaging shoulders backstage at the Democrat de – bait or was that just a dream sequence cartoon blurb above his head showing a whole lotta of hair smelling going on?

My daddy always said the tree of life is like a fruit tree. All the bad rotten fruit falls to the ground, begins to stink then becomes covered with flies. He said it's just like the people that fall off the tree of life; they all become politicians.

My daddy always said left brain, right brain, left hand, right hand, left turn signal, right turn signal, "How hard is that?"

My daddy always said he knew what was for dinner when his mother said we're having poke - rolls and grits. It meant "poke your feet under the table" - "roll your eyes" - "grit your teeth" because the politicians had eaten all the beef that was for dinner.

My daddy always said big print sucks you in and the little print sucks you dry.

My daddy always said if Democrats are following you around sniffing your ass then you didn't clean all the Liberals off of it.

My daddy always said if a woman offers you heaven, don't bend her over and go to hell.

My daddy always said you can tell that Kirsten Gillibrand is the one changing Hillary's diapers and she's learned all the secrets of using bleach to clean her kitty bits.

My daddy always said fake-a-hontas can be seen and heard running up and down the halls of congress screaming, somebody please poke my hontas.

My daddy always said Indian and India scientists were amazed at the size of a buffalo hump in the belly of Hillary Clinton and camel humps on her butt cheeks, but most alarming was the fact she was camel toe free.

My daddy always said before you hit the nail on the head, move your finger.

My daddy always said when you eat a cheesecake does it recycle and come out as chunky cheese? And when you eat a bean burrito does it recycle and come out as another brick in the border wall?

My daddy always said if you don't have grit in your gut then you will never amount to more than a hair on his ass.

My daddy always said Florida is the big nut capital, California is the big butt capital. New York is the Sodom capital, Minnesota is the Gomorrah capital, and Washington, D.C. is their whore.

My daddy always said if you are a midnight toker then you're most likely a daytime loafer.

My daddy always said his life alert call would be... help I farted, and I can't get my wife's foot out of my ass.

My daddy always said when Jennifer Garner petitioned Trump for a national day of mourning for her beloved chicken, Regina George, the world stopped spinning and let her off.

My daddy always said my brother was so dumb that when he told him to shoot the moon, he shot the neighbors ass.

My daddy always said where there is a will there is a way, as-long-as the will leaves you enough money to finance your way.

My daddy always said when you go out on a date with someone and their breath smells like they use their ass to brush their teeth, a good night kiss shouldn't be in the cards.

My daddy always said when you kiss a Democrat on the lips, do you wonder whose 'ass' those lips have been kissing?

My daddy always said if your dog drinks out of the commode and they kiss you, you might as well wipe your ass with your own tongue.

My daddy always said Kim Kardashian's mother said, "Honey, if you build it, it will cumber."

My daddy always said Rosie O'Donnell should have been a Republican as much as she dines in the bushes.

My daddy always said that when Nanny P. weaker of the house found out that one of her underlings actually had a thought, she called in all conferees to investigate who in her house had more than one brain cell.

My daddy always said he couldn't get over the fact he was expected to kiss the lips that had chewed his ass out all day.

My daddy always said a woman should know the difference between tan lines and man lines… which ones to let the sun cross and which ones to let the man cross.

My daddy always said what state were the Salem 'witch' trails held in? That would be "Massachusetts" for you Democrats. Now for the $64,000.00-dollar question… what state is senator fake-a-hontas Warren from? I rest my brain cell.

My daddy always said the advice that Michelle Obama should have given Meghan Markle is have one and be done. After one your ass will only look like the back of a Ford F150 pickup. After two your ass will look like the back of a Mack dump truck like mine.

My daddy always said Al Gore locked everyone's box with bad breath, bad hair, bad B.O., bad gas, and bad speeches.

My daddy always said now that Trump has made fools out of the fools, 'will the fools he made fools out of ever be fooled again?'

My daddy always said Joe 'plugs' Biden is having a heat toke this summer. Senator Harris is spanking his ass with his own words and history. By the time camel toe gets through with smell-yo-hair Joe, he won't have a plug of hair left on his head.

My daddy always said there are three "B's" a woman should not do on a first date – "no beans, no booty and no belching."

My daddy always said if you haven't got time to brush the ants off grandma then you don't need to farm her out to the nursing home because they have the same busy schedule.

My daddy always said A.O.C. a.k.a. 'the tez' has to get her 'ideas' golden showered on before she will learn that there is always someone smarter and there is always someone more powerful and they know when to hold 'em and when to fold 'em.

My Daddy Always Said

My daddy always said the world's greatest recyclers are politicians because they recycle the same old crap every election.

My daddy always said football players want to score, hockey players want an easy puck, and all Tiger Woods wants is to get it in the hole.

My daddy always said good intentions are like a fart. It's gone with the wind 'but' 'butt' actually doing something rather than intending to do something is like the best bowel movement you've ever had. "It feels great! You feel great, and life goes from can't to yes I can!"

My daddy always said that if politicians would just tell the truth 50% of the time then they wouldn't be lying 100% of the time.

My daddy always said if you choose wisely and choose somebody that supports you – you will never have to work a day in your life.

My daddy always said Ross Perot was right in saying that if the voters elected Bill Clinton in 1992, they would hear a sucking sound down south, but the only sucking sound would be from Monica Lewinsky in the oval oral office of the president.

My daddy always said the only difference between hell and hail is when you're in one, you're praying for the other to cool your ass.

My daddy always said the difference between the Bill and a bill is one comes in the mail the other cums in the oval office.

My daddy always said the only difference between liquor and licker is what's in your hands and what's on your tongue.

My daddy always said when Julia Roberts and Sheryl Crow got in a cat fight over who has the most dingle berries on their ass, they couldn't find a judge to get past the smell test.

My daddy always said if you are bad about letting your meat loaf, you will surely wind up with some little meatballs.

My daddy always said it won't hurt one bit if the senators that lose re-election will just swallow their pride and run for the lowly office of congress. Some may even be allowed to carry A.O.C.'s water bottle. The house of representatives needs another flake – then the country could have its own 'flake squad.'

My daddy always said what does a hard-working nurse say to her fellow employees when they invite her out after a twelve-hour shift for a beer – knowing she has a husband that's too lazy to work and three kids waiting on dinner? Sorry ladies, you enjoy the "Millers," at my house, it's Democrat time – "I have to clean, cook, and feed them."

My daddy always said Megan Rapinoe wanted to meet Nancy Pelosi in person so she would know exactly what she'd look like in a couple of years.

My daddy always said when you stop at a roadside stand and get a hot dog, make sure the collar is off before you eat it.

My daddy always said liars, tramps, murderers, thieves, and politicians suddenly become saints when they die.

My daddy always said never buy underwear that's already been to a coo-chie dance.

My daddy always said if you can't pack her, back her or park her - you don't need to be driving her.

My daddy always said life is like a cucumber. You can eat it by itself or put it in a garden salad.

My daddy always said Serena Williams took a chapter out of Hillary Clinton's playbook on how "not" to lose gracefully.

My daddy always said he was on his way to Mount Everest to take a selfie until he found out there wasn't an escalator.

My daddy always said if you get drunk and can't remember your name, the police will remind you who you are not - 'a free bird'.

My daddy always said on the mornings he went to church with his stomach growling and churning, he'd wake up the congregation with his tail hooting louder than a jet engine.

My daddy always said the big difference between tell and tail is smell.

My daddy always said when the house and senate gaveled in for the new session, rules were posted at the doors. Rule number one - if any member has an erection lasting longer than four seconds, notify the surgeon general and get those want nads gone with the wind.

My daddy always said if you are poking Bab's bush with the speed of light then you are a 'racist' 'but' – 'butt' if you are enjoying every stroke of your poke then you are not a 'racist' - you are a slow poker.

My daddy always said if your gut can't hold all the crow you have to eat then keep your mouth shut.

My daddy always said when Opportunity knocks, let her in or she will go back to the strip club.

My daddy always said if you are in a new church and the pastor says we will let the newest member pick the next three hymns don't stand up, look around and say I'll pick him, him, and him.

My daddy always said what's the difference between a snowflake and a corn flake? That depends on whether you ask Jeff Flake or Elijah Cummings and what time of the month it is for them, maxi or mini.

My daddy always said there is not a woman alive that likes a racist poker. Unless, she is a hooker and she is hoping for that one stroke and done.

My daddy always said if you are about to give your cat an enema makes sure your life insurance is paid up.

My daddy always said since Oregon lost its beaver status of not producing any beavers for the presidential race, can we give that honor to Hawaii for producing Tulsi Gabbard?

My daddy always said if you want to learn the difference between hold and hole call the 1-800 customer helpline with a problem. You will die and be buried in a hole before you get off hold.

My daddy always said politicians have been drinking too much of their ego – because now they are trying to piss all their lies into the ears of voters.

My daddy always said the best thing about a farmer's daughter is she can't keep her calves together.

My daddy always said roses are red, violets are blue, but money is green and if you don't want to work then screw you.

My daddy always said life is like a fuzzball. You begin from just a speck of dust then you grow through life until God vacuums you up.

My daddy always said a Milton, Georgia farmer, who says his miniature ass was literally scared to death by July 4th fireworks, has been invited to bring his new ass along with some fireworks to Elijah's Baltimore. He has a plan to rid the city of ass size rodents before hollow wieners hit the streets for tricks and treats.

My daddy always said when somebody you know doesn't believe in the 'here after' take them out to sea about 20 miles and say, if you are not here after what I'm here after, you're going to be here after I'm gone.

My daddy always said if you are spending your time looking at the southend of a northbound donkey, it's time for you to find some new ass.

My daddy always said if you have an erection lasting less than four seconds you are one of the good guys according to the Democrats.

My daddy always said what did the pool lifeguard say to the pool pooping fecal Fein who left a back-booty log bruiser in the shallow end? Snowflakes and flies – snowflakes and flies, the more I see snowflakes, the more I like flies.

My daddy always said if people are given the chance to choose between being an ass or a hole most Democrats choose ass. They never stop to think they can always dig their way out of a hole, but they can never dig their way out of being an ass.

My daddy always said buying used false teeth is like buying a used jockstrap. You have no idea when to start the gag meter.

My daddy always said what did America get when ro-bot Mueller testified before congress? They got Schultz from Hogan's Heros – I know nothing – I see nothing – I hear nothing – I speak nothing.

My daddy always said the only regular thing you could count on at the old folk's home was prune smelling air biscuits.

My daddy always said if you have a goat and it smells like Paris then stop that goat from eating at the Hilton.

My daddy always said Elizabeth Warren was a fake Indian standing at the college door where she fell in love with the free tuition money over at the government store. E-lie-a-beth – E-lie-a-beth, pointed to her high cheek bones, while singing give-me – give-me – gime – gime mo-money. Don't you just love this free gov-ment! Money that you can get with a 'fake I identity' from the gov-ment store. Vote for me E-lie-a-beth so I can get more gov-ment money – from the gov-ment store.

My daddy always said you've got them himorhoids and them herorhoids and you never want to mix them with ass-ta-rhoids.

My daddy always said take the feathers from my hair, rub some bear grease in it, I don't care. It's election time, my brain is out of school. It's okay if I act a damn fool. I was going to do cartwheels in a beaded leather dress across the debate stage until I bent over and my back reminded me of my age. So now, I'll just do like Jerry Nadler and waddle – waddle. Please support your local poke-a-hontas.

My daddy always said Nancy Pelosi was running barefooted through broken glass up to the White House just to chew out the president's ass for disrupting the squad of four that she had under control after changing their diapers and burping them while waiting on the three brain cells she ordered off dBay so each one of the squad could have their very own brain cell.

My daddy always said never buy a monkey that's dead – never live with anyone that's not well-read – and never, ever wake up in Robert Mueller's bed.

C. Birdfinger

My daddy always said a wink, or a nod is the same to a blind man.

My daddy always said the only difference between a one and a two is a one.

My daddy always said there is a bill before both houses of congress to stop a Chinese manufacturing company from marketing and selling car window stickers that read 'depends' for ass of elephant or donkey.

My daddy always said when it comes to Elijah Cumming's district of Baltimore, Trump should do the right thing. Hire all the illegal Mexicans, build a containment wall around the district and ship it to China. Let them kill and eat all the rats then ship Baltimore back. Problem solved except for it still being a hell hole.

My daddy always said when it comes to insuring that - that is 'that' you can't take anything away from 'that' or that. 'That' is what represents 'that' – given that – that isn't 'that' morsel of sanity that doesn't flow between the ears of politicians - 'that's called common sense.

My Daddy Always Said

My daddy always said if you go to work before you can and work until after you can't, you will achieve what the Democrats want, "yo money."

My daddy always said peanut butter is a double choker. It will choke you up going in and it will choke you up going out.

My daddy always said if you let a fool have a gun, then you have a fool with a gun.

My daddy always said what did President Trump say to Elijah Cummings when he 'woke' the Democrat representative of Baltimore Maryland? "You've got male – rats, you've got female – rats, you've got dead rats" - congress – mun, you have rodents. Congressman Cummings, 'what we have here is failure to do the right thing' for your district.

My daddy always said it's a short drive from your ass to your brain. Why else do you think the liberals walk around with their heads up their asses?

My daddy always said the only reason the southern belle was disqualified from the beauty pageant was she wore a yellow bikini with the words 'miss' on the back and 'sippime' on the front.

My daddy always said a politician doesn't care who you vote for as long as you vote for them.

My daddy always said what did Patriots owner Robert Kraft say to the judge? "Your honor, I can promise you this Chinese thing will never happen again. Next time I'll use the Russians to get my collusion on."

My daddy always said there are two things you'll never know, if there's lice in your rice or bugs in your beans.

My daddy always said there's only two times a day a politician will lie; one is during the dark of night, the other is in the light of day.

My daddy always said there are some gov-ment teats that half the world would love to be suckling on and the other half would be frying in a pan of envy. Hello 'Tulsi' a 10 + 10 + 10 + 10 + 10 and again and again and again.

My daddy always said dishes and dreams are alike; both can be shattered by carelessness.

My daddy always said the best laxative for constipation is to get caught in a two-hour traffic jam.

My daddy always said there should be a movie about the rats and rodents of hell hole Maryland A.K.A. Baltimore, Maryland. You could have Elijah Cummings play himself – 'Boss Rat.' You could have A.O.C. star as 'Dat Rat' and don't forget Nancy Pelosi who would be 'Mutha Rat' ruler of all the hell hole rats and rodents. They could all build empires. Hire Jussie Smollet to design their turfs with his broad knowledge of staging fake attacks. Jussie could bring the grand duchess of 'fakes,' fake-a- hontas Warren. Maybe she could get that mosquito to return her one drop of Indian blood so she could declare 'boss rats' hell hole a fake-a-hontas reservation. Then she could start selling rat and rodents sight-seeing tours to the Chinese since their massage parlors are off limits to N.F.L. owners and everybody knows they need all the jobs Americans won't do.

My daddy always said when there are 10 toes up and 10 toes down with two asses moving round and round, "it's not called a coincidence."

My daddy always said when you reach the age where there's more hair on your ass than your head, it's not called the Age of Aquarius.

My daddy always said until the dark days of death, I will suffer without rest. They will hunt and haunt my very soul. Liberties will be taken – truths will never be told. Then the world will discover that I was only a disguised Democrat. That's my story and I'm sticking 'it' to you, 'so' "that's that," you Mississippi Re-pub-li-cant's. "Camp Ben – A - Dick Waller."

My daddy always said never grow a beak and peck **it with the chickens. Never throw Caution to the wind, if she weighs more than a hundred pounds. Never pull the hair out of somebody else's nose and never, ever use toe jam to make a peanut butter and jam sandwich.

My daddy always said when Marianne Williamson was asked by the fake news what in her educational background qualified her to be president of the United States? Without hesitation, her answer was, 'I have graduated cum – loudly in everything I have ever done.'

My daddy always said there is a time to remember and a time to forget but there is never a time to forget what you need to remember.

My daddy always said where were you on that November day when the world stopped turning and Hillary lost? Did you and Jeremiah help her drink the wine? Everybody knows Jeremiah always had some mighty fine wine.

My daddy always said the writing was on the wall. I've been good – I've been bad. You'll never get what I had. I've walked among the stars. I've had donors who thought they were from Mars. You'll never know what ever I've had but the pokes and chokes in the oval office was not bad. So put your morals in check – no – no – on second thought, put that check in the mail because of Jeffrey Epstein, I may need it for bail.

My daddy always said when your breath smells like burnt hair and turd salad you shouldn't expect a good morning kiss.

My daddy always said in life, never build a road you're not willing to travel on – in both directions.

My daddy always said there are no rules for how often to take a bath but once a day is a good place to start.

My daddy always said there is absolutely no difference between Democrats and squirrels, they both love nuts.

My daddy always said if given a choice between maggots and politicians, always choose maggots because at least you'll know what you're getting.

My daddy always said there is never anyone in the way of your success but you.

My daddy always said when your stomach is full, and your head is empty – your feeding the wrong body part.

My daddy always said – oh say can you pee - Nancy is thirstee – she has been chasing the rodents and rats and four hellcats that won't let her rest and do what she does best, 'nothing' absolutely nothing. Say it again, 'nothing.' Wake her when her term is over.

My daddy always said a roll in the hay is one sure way to check for allergies.

My daddy always said when love conquers all, everyone will have wings and live on streets paved with gold.

My daddy always said it is far better to achieve any goal than to have never had any goals.

My daddy always said everybody is right some of the time, but nobody is right all the time, unless they sign your check.

My daddy always said when you are working for minimum wage, every day is hump day.

My daddy always said the weatherman said because of the excessive heat don't walk your dogs on asphalt or concrete pavement - but – butt – gave no advice on walking your barefooted grandma on either concrete or asphalt. 'Poor grandma never gets any love.' Are those ants on grandma that you didn't have time to brush off?

My daddy always said if the shoe fits buy it. If it doesn't fit don't buy it. If life fits, live it – if life doesn't fit, change it.

My daddy always said happy people aren't lazy and lazy people aren't happy – happy people love life – lazy people don't have a life.

My daddy always said he fell in love with my mother because of what was in her jeans.

My daddy always said if she has too many fingers in her pie you shouldn't be the one eating her pie.

My daddy always said if you think life is a bowl of cherries, try eating that bowl of cherries and see where your gut and butt keep you running to all day.

C. Birdfinger

My daddy always said as he 'ate' this whole damn buffet of ignorance from birth in order to become a Democrat did 'Representative Steve Cohen' pay for the Colonel's bucket of Kentucky Fried Chicken like 'Maxine Waters' taxpayers payed? Speaking of taxpayers, why didn't you eat Church's Fried Chicken or Popeye's Fried Chicken or Chic-Fil-A's Chicken? "Are you a racist?" Why not tacos? Why not chitlins? Why not Chinese – why? Why? Why? Did you have to eat Jennifer Garner's dead chicken, Steven Cohen, why?

My daddy always said his two greatest inventions never made it to the As Seen on TV shelves. The first being jalapeno hemorrhoid ointment the second being a barbwire thong.

My daddy always said trying to find lucidity in the government is like trying to light the world with luciferin flies.

My daddy always said Joe "Blo" and Snowflake – A – Hontas both should set a good example. They are both white – both want to be the supreme leader so therefore both could be considered white Supremes. Now all they need is Diana Ross to sing ain't no Democrat high enough.

My daddy always said food for thought is never free.

My daddy always said when the farts of your head lice wake you up at night, it's time to debug your head.

My daddy always said when the booger you pull out of your nose is bigger than your nose you are way past the expiration date for harvesting your boogers.

My daddy always said when your ass and stomach are the same distance from the floor you have couch disease.

My daddy always said there's three B's on your body that rule your life. … your breasts, your belly, and your butt because they're always reaching for the ground.

My daddy always said you are who you are and if you give that up for somebody then you are who they are.

My daddy always said when you carry a chip on your shoulder with malice in your head – you will never be happy until you are dead.

My daddy always said the reason Taylor Swift didn't endorse Hillary Clinton for president was she wasn't 'woke.' By the time she was 'woke' Hillary was one 'toke' over the line and Donald Trump had reduced her to drinking 'Mad Dog 20-20 wine.'

My daddy always said what is the best flea, fly, tick and Democrat repellant? M.A.G.A. hats with Off – on your head.

My daddy always said if all you can afford is watermelon wine then don't order a shrimp cocktail.

My daddy always said if you are a fickle person you are always one chorus away from a goodbye lullaby.

My daddy always said if your door is always open and somebody's sleeping bag is always behind your couch then your road is not less traveled.

My daddy always said when your weapon is your mouth remember you can't reload the words that come out.

My daddy always said it's better to have your feet on the ground than your head up your ass.

My daddy always said no matter how poor you are, everybody wants more. The government wants more taxes, the politicians wants more perks, the preacher wants more fried chicken, the boss wants more work, and the wife wants more poke.

My daddy always said if you know what you're doing, and you know where you're going then why the hell do you always call somebody for help when the jail doors lock behind you?

My daddy always said some people don't know the difference between debate and debait 'but' there is always hope for you comrade Bernie and Mayor – who will never be a major player.

My daddy always said never smell the used underwear at a garage sale.

My daddy always said when Hillary came out of the closet and identified as a presidential looser all the voters chanted no-mas, no mas, no mas.

My daddy always said when he was growing up, beer nuts and deer nuts were both under a buck.

My daddy always said if you're out hiking never use pinecones for toilet paper.

My daddy always said if you are alive and they are dead, bury them in a private cemetery in your head then get back on the bicycle of life and pedal on.

My daddy always said if you can't sleep and you are up all night – don't waste all that time. Get a night job to go with that day job.

My daddy always said live with the living before you sleep with the dead.

My daddy always said when you get a kink in your colon - by any means end the logjam. For nothing feels finer than to empty your behiner.

My daddy always said the snowflakes found Marianne Williamson in the outhouse platting her under arm hair while spanking her monkey between spider barks. Singing one toke over the line, if only Hillary would share a glass of her Mad Dog 20-20 wine to help get me another poke before the end of time.

My daddy always said some gastrointestinal doctors have issued a warning that intentional and deliberately inhaling contents of Democrats colon ass gas can be harmful or fatal. Gas mask are available on barf-bay or you can get a free gov-ment one from the capital of "rats and rodents," the city of Ball-tied-more-on you.

My daddy always said if you haven't walked a mile in someone else's shoes it's probably because you haven't been drunk enough yet.

My daddy always said when he was a boy, he ate so many Moon pies that his ass was in a constant state of eclipse.

My daddy always said the only difference between a movie star and a politician is one lies and acts when the camera is on and the other does the same when the camera is on or off.

My Daddy Always Said

My daddy always said with everything and everyone there is a rhyme and a reason. The reason you can't rhyme is you never took the time to learn the difference between reason and rhyme. My daddy always said shining a light on a problem doesn't help if the light is dimwitted.

My daddy always said the measure of a man is the same as a woman - from the top of their head to the bottom of their feet.

My daddy always said when you go to a title loan place for a loan and there is one hand shaking your hand and another on your ass, just bend over because you're about to be screwed.

My daddy always said when your mind is on your money and your money is on your mind - your love life will get left behind.

C. Birdfinger

My daddy always said when you are falling head over heels in love, land feet first so you can run for your life.

My daddy always said the reason demo is in the word Democrat is God wanted you to try out being one before you became one.

My daddy always said when he took a survey on who was the craziest one of all', every finger pointed back at him.

My daddy always said when he came home and discovered Alice didn't live there anymore, he let Lucy move in.

My daddy always said Elizabeth fake-a-hontas Warren is pissed off at Christopher Columbus for not discovering her camel toe.

My daddy always said if politicians exercised their brains half as much as they exercise their mouths our country wouldn't be broke and fat.

My daddy always said inquiring minds want to know if Beto and his wife ate their babies' turds on texas toast – white bread toast – brown bread toast – avocado toast – raisin bread toast or just sun-dried cow patty style.

My daddy always said the only reason Taylor Swift came out of the closet as a Democrat is because she wanted the world to know she is a 'demo - rat - too!'

My daddy always said don't get your margarita salt from the bartender's armpits.

My daddy always said Elijah was the boss rat who ruled over Baltimore. He fell in love with the rich Washington Democrats who lived next door. The po folks in the 'less' not 'more' fought the rats as best as they could. With little or no help from boss rat they soon gave up on the hood and let the rats rule.

My daddy always said doctors have discovered a cure for him-roids and her-roids "don't vote for dem-o-rats."

My daddy always said, what's in your wallet? Nothing, absolutely nothing – say it again, nothing. Between the hackers, the slackers, the snowflakes, the Jeff Flakes and the demon – crats, there is no capital. Everyone is just hoping that comrade Bernie Sanders will drop just a few of his communist millions into a soup kitchen collection plate so everyone can stop eating poke – rolls and grits.

My daddy always said Senator fake-a-hontas Warren was stopped by T.S.A. and questioned for having beads, blankets, and a flying carpet. When asked why she answered, "You can't leave anything to chance or Trump when claiming Indian blood."

My daddy always said Kim Kardashian is uncoupling from Kanye West because she can't keep dragging two assholes around.

My daddy always said he was fired from the best job he ever had for sticking his finger in the sausage grinder and she was fired for letting him.

My daddy always said the only reason Senator Dianne Feinstein picked Ford to testify before the Senate was because she wanted the world to know there is somebody uglier than her.

My daddy always said Al Roker was overheard asking his ego, "Does my ass make Mount Everest look small?"

My daddy always said when you are in a deep depression between somebody's legs, don't tweet about it to her husband.

My daddy always said there once was a middle leg whose name was peg, who never had to bend or beg, for even former presidents are smart enough to know, you can't put a liberal pig in a conservative hole.

My daddy always said when hurricane Maxine came ashore in California, Al Roker reported to Lester Holt, "I'm standing knee-deep in Maxine's Waters. No one, and I mean no one in California can escape the murky-stale-stanky Waters of Maxine."

My daddy always said why is it against the law to feed stray cats and stray dogs in Ohio and not against the law to feed stray illegal aliens? Sounds like this state just hates animals.

My daddy always said when Bill discovered that all the hosts of The View were from the Bay of Pigs all he could say was, "Oink-oink."

My daddy always said never buy pre skid-marked underwear.

My daddy always said some people sell their souls for fame, some people sell their souls for fortune, but Jeff Flake sold his soul for Democrats on the dollar.

My daddy always said the liberals honored Hillary Clinton for lying in state. Unidentified sources report that there's not a single state that she didn't lie in… but what difference does it make now.

My daddy always said the Democrats motto is - don't ask us any questions if you don't want to hear any lies.

My daddy always said never play food detective by lifting your dog's tail or your wife's leg and smelling their asses to find out which one ate your pizza.

My daddy always said never be like Alissa Milano and put the dingle berries from your ass in your breakfast cereal and call it "Raising Brains".

My daddy always said Nancy Pee-loosely keep saying "we" when a reporter stated: Speaker, you're standing there all alone. Why do you keep saying 'we'? Pee-loosely replied, "I have some dingle berries in my hip pocket that were just elected."

My daddy always said farts have three classifications: no scent, not too stinky, and gag me… gut wrenching… dead skunk smelling fart. He suggested never, 'ever,' naming a fart before giving birth to it.

My daddy always said that the U.S. Congress should pass a law requiring all politicians to wear a sign on their backs saying: Warning, stay back 100 feet. My ass gas is not green gas it's racist gas. It races from my gut to my butt and out to your nose.

My daddy always said some people will fo-cus on a happy new year, some people will fo-cus on the new year, and some people will just fu – cup the year.

My daddy always said the only difference between the snowflakes and Jeff Flake is one is a lunatic and the others are Luditics.

My daddy always said Nancy Pee-loosely sings the old Captain and Tennille songs to Trump. "Love will keep us together if you do that to my muskrat one more time."

My daddy always said Trump will have to adjust to "S. P. A. M." - I. E. "Speaker - Pelosi – Americas - Mistake" for the next two years.

My daddy always said when the mosquito bit Elizabeth Warren and drank her only drop of Indian blood, she lost her Native American support.

My daddy always said never use your dandruff for your chocolate cupcakes sprinkles.

My daddy always said Whoopi and Joy didn't dilly dally around. They went straight from love handles to lard ass handles in record time.

My daddy always said the producers of The View should have to get a tent zoning ordinance since most of its hosts wear tents.

My daddy always said after a rear end collision prep-h is preferred over a one call that's all attorney, who will only dig deeper in your ass for his one turd of yo-money.

My daddy always said slick Willie said the best thing that happened to him while he was president was playing poke-her face with Monica Lewinsky.

My daddy always said when Hillary was asked to buy a brick with her name on it to support Trumps border wall – Hilda-Beast asked, "Are you frigging crazy? My name has been on every shit house wall in the world and not once did I have to pay a dime. Besides, if I know Trump, he'll put not only my name but my face on that brick. Then he'll build an outhouse, put my brick at the bottom of the hole face up, and have a reality show called - Who Wants to Turd Bomb Hillary?"

My daddy always said there are himoroids, heroroids, asteroids and assroids but the most famous roid of all is Hildaroid.

My daddy always said do you or someone you know have a bad case of hemorrhoids from sitting on your lazy ass waiting on the govment? There is help for you after all. Call for your money at-a-turney 1-800-ax-man to get them 'roids' on the chopping block. Remember, 1-ax- that's − max or 1 − chop − that's all.

My daddy always said in Angelina Jolie's divorce papers they discovered the reason she divorced Brad. He was born a vegan and she needed more meat to thrive and survive as a woman.

My daddy always said Thanksgiving grace like this, "In the name of the Father, the Son, and the Holy Ghost, whoever eats the fastest will get the most!"

My daddy always said Hillary is suing Al Gore because when he unlocked his lockbox, he ate all the tacos and drank all the Boones Farm wine and all she got was losing two presidential races.

My daddy always said scientists on board the space station have pinpointed the cause of global warming with the help of infrared imaging. The biggest culprit is the enormous planet size ass of Al Gore.

My daddy always said he waited all his life to hear those magic words from a woman… "back up." He just never expected to hear them from a doctor with both hands on his shoulders.

My daddy always said there should be a litmus test every January for all elected politicians to see if they are brain-dead.

My daddy always said that Kim Kardashian has renamed her ass Las Vegas because she hopes what happens in Las Vegas, stays in Las Vegas.

My daddy always said what did Anthony's 'Weiner' say to his brain? "Dead or alive you're cumming with me."

My daddy always said when he went to the doctor complaining of long-dong fever, the doctor ordered the nurse to give him a couple of ass burns.

My daddy always said the one and only reason Trump signed a budget bill on Friday, March 29th was to get the keys back for the White House that Nancy and Chuck had taken away.

My daddy always said Whoopi and Joy's daily View wardrobe is provided by Guess. Guess what tent they are wearing today?

My daddy always said when a fart is more than wind don't be a fool and fart again.

My daddy always said if Pink married Lady Gaga would she be known as Pink Lady Gaga or just Pink Lady?

My daddy always said his fourth wife lived in Palm bitch Florida while he was living in kiss-sa-her ass Florida.

My daddy always said "Taylor" has been on Ellen. "Taylor" has been on Oprah, but "Taylor" still hasn't found anybody who wants to be on "Taylor."

My daddy always said if you wake up one day with corns on your feet, next time just plant beans.

My daddy always said the fur-cast for the vacant spot Kathie Lee Gifford is making (with all the knives in her back and feet up her ass) will be decided by who has the brownest nose and whose lips can be pried off the Big Kahuna's ass.

My Daddy Always Said

My daddy always said there's one mosquito flying around out there that's a full blooded native American mosquito after drinking that one drop of Indian blood from fake-a-hontas Warren.

My daddy always said Bella Star has something the world wanted to see. Whoopi has nothing anybody wants to see.

My daddy always said when you're standing knee-deep in life's problems start praying for longer legs.

My daddy always said a sardines and beer fart will leave a last impression on a first date.

My daddy always said if you get a frog stuck in your throat it only means you didn't chew that sucker long enough before you tried to swallow it.

My daddy always said Colonel Sanders is crying crab apple tears because Jennifer Garner wasted a perfectly good dead chicken by burying it in the cold, hard ground instead of frying it up.

My daddy always said what happens at the north pole stays at the north "pole" but what happened at the ass "hole" came out as Michael Moore.

My daddy always said if you are not happy with your gut wagon then back away from the buffet.

My daddy always said Oprah should be given a medal for being smart enough not to interview liar – liar pants on fire Empire actor Jussie Smollet.

My daddy always said his daddy said when he was growing up if you had to buy fertilizer for your garden that meant you had an indoor toilet.

My daddy always said when a squirrel eats your nuts you become a fake-a- hontas Warren or an Alexandria Ocasio Cortez or even worse, Virginia Governor Ralph Northam.

My daddy always said after all the books that were bought for you and all the teachers that taught you ** it and you still can't pass third grade--- there is always gov-ment jobs – that's jobs with four letters 'but' your Democrat Uncle Joe spelled jobs with just three letters – no third grade diploma for you Joe.

My daddy always said if humans sniffed asses like dogs, it would take someone a week to sniff all of Oprah's ass.

My daddy always said that the only reason he didn't slap the truth out of the biggest lie of all was because he couldn't catch the damn thing! Everybody knows that a lie spreads faster than a California wildfire, but a snail can outrun the truth.

My daddy always said when Nancy Pee Loosely was reelected Speaker of the House for the second time, making history, she failed to keep decorum – decency – dignity – etiquette. In short, she was elected speaker of the "rats" Democrats = dem-rats. Kevin McCarthy was elected leader of the "cans" = Republi "cans" but McCarthy can't get the cans out of the can - so the rats are running wild and have taken over the house. There are rat turds everywhere, some screaming impeach! While the whole country knows they don't have two brain cells each.

My daddy always said without a shadow of a doubt there is heaven on earth and hell on earth. It's noted that when looking at Nancy Pelosi's face – that's looking at hell. It's also noted that when looking at Tulsi Gabbard's face – that is looking at heaven.

My daddy always said Nancy Pelosi said Mr. Trump, here is an idea. Let's run it up your ass and see if it flies. "No damn wall!" I don't have a wall around my ass and nobody, I mean nobody, has ever even tried to get near my ass.

My daddy always said never shake hands with someone who just walked out of a toilet stall.

My daddy always said the only difference between a "walking bull" and "talking bull," is words and turds.

My daddy always said what did the only poor old Republican woman in the city of Baltimore say when she called the help line? "Help! Help! I've farted and I hear the demon – rats coming, coming for to carry me to the first ever rat and rodent feast. Will they go green or will they bar-b-que or bake? Will they put an apple in my mouth? Will they use an oven or a grill? I know I'm old, but dem Democrats should just let this grandma watch Netflix and chill."

My daddy always said some people can wear leggings and some people wear jeggings, but you have the cast of a talk show, The View, who can only wear teggings. That's tents with holes for the head and arms.

My daddy always said life is like a bad dream that keeps repeating itself. You wake up- you use the potty- you shower- you eat- you go to school or work- you eat- you come home- you eat- you go to the potty- you shower- you go to bed- and repeat- and repeat- and repeat- till you die.

My daddy always said while the two nuns from a catholic school in Torrance, California stole over a half million dollars to gamble in Las Vegas, inquiring minds want to know, which one was the him and which one was the her? Or were they both just like, "It's good to be an American! – God bless the U.S.A."

My daddy always said he was injured when a lawyer struck him from behind with both hands… in his wallet.

My daddy always said the answer to the age-old question, how do you get into a foxhole is 'you raise its tail.'

My daddy always said when he was a young man, he loved married women because married women didn't yell, they didn't tell, they didn't swell, and they were grateful as hell.

My daddy always said Monica Lewinsky's favorite part of the song Southbound and Down is, "I'm going to do what other interns won't."

My daddy always said there are only two people in the history of the world responsible for glo-belly warming, Marilyn Monroe and Elvis Presley. There's not a barn, bathroom, or bedroom that they didn't heat up with their images on peoples brain.

My daddy always said when two gold leopards were filmed running through the jungle in Kenner, Louisiana it was determined to be a hoax. It was only Al Sharpton and Jesse Jackson chasing a dollar that slick Willie and James Carvel were dragging through a trailer park.

My daddy always said when a lunatic goes crazy that's when you have the birth of a Democrat.

My daddy always said a redheaded possum is as rare as a chicken with teeth.

My daddy always said what did Rihanna say to the press when she moved back in with Chris Brown? "And the beat-down goes on."

My daddy always said when John Smith founded Jamestown, Virginia in 1607 it wasn't long before he was poking – hontas.

My daddy always said when fake-a-hontas was young and in her prime, Running Bear could have had her on her knees at any time. Now that she is old and lost her American Indian D.N.A. even James Carvel won't drag a dollar bill her way.

My daddy always said if you are a Democrat you may have U.A.B. - Under Achieved Brain. The prescribed remedy is have a Republican give you a swift kick in the ass to loosen one of your brain cells.

My daddy always said the only thing that comes out of a politicians' mouth is butt waste.

My daddy always said when it comes to the odd couple of Nancy Pee Loosely and Chuck-U-Schumer, everyone but Chuckie knows who has the only set of balls. And she knows when, where and how to use them-thar- balls.

My daddy always said never trust anybody that lives outside of your head.

My daddy always said the world knows fake-a-hontas Warren has "horns". What the world needs now is to see her forked tongue and war dance.

My daddy always said the only difference between Listerine and Irene is one gives you good breath and the other gives you a good night.

My daddy always said if hope was piss, we would all drown.

My daddy always said never bend over when a politician is around unless you like getting screwed.

My daddy always said toll roads and hemorrhoids are not alike. One you pay to drive on, the other you pray to sit on.

My daddy always said everybody has two corn holes. One where the corn goes in, the other one where the corn comes out.

My daddy always said any hands crawling up his leg can have a ball.

My daddy always said Joy Behar has never been beautiful in white face or Halloween black face. She was never beautiful at nine or twenty-nine. She looks like the love child of James Carvel and Danny DeVito who came out after an enema.

My daddy always said there is a law in Assland that reads, if it hurts – squirts or wears a saddle, moos or chews grass, stay out of that ass. That goes for you goat lovers, too.

My daddy always said Jussie Smollett proved you can hire non-American citizens to do the work that honest Americans just won't do.

My daddy always said Mr. President there are Democrats on your shoulders, they have you bloodied and bruised. They have you cornered; maybe too weak to fight. Will you be America's Rocky or will you, Mr. President, with all those demon – crats on our shoulders just grab your ankles and bend over?

My daddy always said if the president would only put A.O.C. in charge of the illegal invasion they would all self-deport when they see her zero I. Q. at work.

My daddy always said Gov. Ralph Northam thanked Jussie Smollett and Al Gore for taking the media heat off him and his black face in K.K.K. yearbook photos.

My daddy always said when his ass and brain went into a collusion, he always wound up changing his diaper.

My daddy always said when life gives you hemorrhoids get Prep H. When life gives you lice, get lice shampoo. When life gives you a Democrat, get a divorce.

My daddy always said when he could find two brain cells to rub together, he could come up with some of the best insults- outsults- downsults- eastsults- westsults- leftsults- rightsults, along with a maze of pollywogs.

My daddy always said bad breath and stinking farts are the matches that light the fires of separation.

My daddy always said knock-knock! Who's there? The professor. Professor who? The professor who told Alexandria Ocasio Cortez that what we have here is 'failure to educate.'

My daddy always said the Chinese have come up with another scheme to get 'their money' out of your pocket. It's called a heavy blanket.

My daddy always said Democrat Governor Ralph Northam of Virginia ran a successful Demon - cratic campaign with the slogan, "Vote for me, get yo babies killed for free."

My daddy always said since scientists have discovered a cream that will remove eye bags, Alexandria Ocasio Cortez, the newly elected one brain cell Congresswoman, wants to know if the cream will remove the old bags in Congress.

My daddy always said after he literally worked his ass off, his teeth fell out, his hair turned white. Then he couldn't find anybody to share his farts with at night.

My daddy always said the best cure for dry scalp is standing in the rain.

My daddy always said if Beto O'Rouke could get Hildabeast to loan him the Monica Lewinsky thong that she confiscated from slick Willie's collection and Beto could get Oprah to wear it while dancing at his campaign stops, he might get more than two assholes and four elbows to show up.

My daddy always said the definition of agony of de-feet is wearing shoes two sizes too small.

My daddy always said what did the doctors say when Nancy Pelosi went in for an emergency colonoscopy? "Houston, we have a polyp! No, wait, that's just Jerrold Nadler having lunch."

My daddy always said when in the can - place your elbows on your knees, first a little grunt then a big squeeze, that's how you get rid of those demon-d's.

My daddy always said Oprah was heard at a Beto O'Rourke campaign rally saying, "You get a hope, and you get a hope, and you get a hope. It's all because, as you three people that attended this fiasco know, Obama kept all the change and the Clintons kept all the folding money, so all you get is hope."

My daddy always said everybody is famous for the song On the Road Again, but Hillary Clinton is famous for being on the losing end again and again and again.

My daddy always said doctors have discovered why Democrat Representative Adam Schiff has a stretched pencil neck and bobble head. E. M. T.'s nearly pulled his head off, getting it out of Ukraine billionaire Biden's ass.

My daddy always said the reason everything is big in Texas is that's where Napoleon beat his bone apart.

My daddy always said Senator Elizabeth Warren was caught at the little big horn flea market trying to buy a drop of Indian blood so she wouldn't be known as fake-a-hontas.

My daddy always said all politicians have I.B.S., 'involuntary – butt – smooching.'

My daddy always said everybody that's breathing, and has more than one brain cell has heard of 'the old wives' tale' but – butt, what happens to 'the new wives' tail?' After the expiration date, and they become old wives will they get the forty-acre ass -reparation or the ten-dollar tube of ass restoration?

My daddy always said if the woodpecker's pecker pecks wood what does man's pecker peck?

My daddy always said a gallon of porcupine piss is worth every penny you paid for it.

My daddy always said if only the Democrats could get Trump out and put A.O.C. in as president then fake-a-hontas Warren could be vice president. Then A.O.C. could borrow Monica Lewinsky's thong and dance for the 'Dick – Tater' Kim Jong Un in her borrowed thong while fake-a-hontas Warren played her Indian "heritage" drum. And all the world would be green, and all the Republicans would stop being mean.

My daddy always said once you win the battle of constipation you can sit on the throne.

My daddy always said when D-Fi's old Ford ran out of water and began to overheat at the Senate hearing, Maxine Waters was overheard saying, "This country doesn't need another 'fake-a-hontas,' just let the witch melt."

My daddy always said when you are ordering a product – 'operators are standing by to help,' but when you have a problem with that product - you are on your own.

My daddy always said when someone steps on your grave, fart real loud.

My daddy always said when you are about to propose make sure there are no boogers hanging out your nose.

My daddy always said Fox News network hired the first anchor, looking like a Chupacabra, to host a show when they hired Donna Breazeale.

My daddy always said you can't fix stupid; but you can elect it to public office.

My daddy always said when A.O.C. was told her green new deal forbid her from flying or riding in a car, A.O.C. grabbed her trusted red Russian made bicycle, started riding away and was immediately arrested for peddling hope and change without being elected president.

My daddy always said the U.S. Senate and the U.S. Congress had to hire doctors to determine which of their members has a lead ass or just a dead ass.

My daddy always said the only difference between him-o-roids and her-o-roids is the spelling.

My daddy always said when a fat cat Hollywood actor was asked whose boots has your ass been polishing in D.C. he replied, "Nobody. Democrats don't know how-to put-on boots."

My daddy always said if you know the difference between right and wrong and you always do right then you will never be at the wrong place at the wrong time.

My daddy always said politics is a game of chance, checkers, and chess. So, what do the Republicans need to do while the fire is hot? Trade U.S. Representative Steve King of Iowa who the 'Republicans hate' for Tulsi Gabbard U.S. representative from Hawaii who the 'Democrats hate.' After Tulsi spanked the Democrats darling Kamala Harris, exposing her 'checkered past,' the Republicans could 'play chess' with their old buddy Steve King. Both parties could take a 'chance' and meet on the fifty-yard line to trade tat for tit.

My daddy always said the Democrats don't know what they don't know, and the Republicans are refusing to buy them any more books and teach them how to read. Now the Democrats are left with scraping the bottom of the barrel for any sign of 'intelligence.' They struck out with A.O.C.

My daddy always said there's only one difference between nude and naked. If you're from the North someone is nude and if you're from the South someone is naked.

My daddy always said when he passed a dump truck with a handwritten sign on the back that read, "I am an ass-fault driver for the city. I drive the main roads passing by all the potholes that were caused by – cronyism – nepotism – racialism and don't care "ism" and the last line said it all. Wake me when it's quitting time."

My daddy always said when the pee-ew scale hits 10, don't pass go, don't go to jail, get your stinking ass in the bathroom and wash that tail.

My daddy always said drinking decaf coffee is like eating the beans without the pork, farting without a smell, taking change out of the collection plate or showing up pregnant on your first date. Somebody else got the meat – all you got were the potatoes.

My daddy always said Mississippi lawmaker State Representative Doug McLeod of Lucedale, who was arrested for assaulting his wife because she wouldn't undress for sex – said, "I married her for better or worse and when she wouldn't give up the better then I gave her the worse."

My daddy always said the only difference between old nags and old hags is one wears a halter and has four legs, the other wears a dress and never shaves her legs.

My daddy always said when Hillary was being interviewed for her farewell memoir, she was asked what she learned in the eight years she spent at the White House that fulfilled her life to which she replied, "I learned how to churn my own butter."

My daddy always said fee-mal-`e senators and fee-mal-`e congresswomen have formed a class action lawsuit against evolution for being born without a camel toe.

My daddy always said when you are in the lead you have finally got the lead out of your ass.

My daddy always said what does a fart say when it's born? I've got to get out of this ass even if it's the last thing I ever do.

My daddy always said never shake hands with someone who just wiped their nose 'with that hand.'

My daddy always said when the Democrat reporter was asked to describe Jerry Nad -lie -er, the reporter said he is short, fat, and squatty... all ass and nobody.

My daddy always said there are two things you never do while playing in the sand, wipe your eyes and wipe your ass.

My daddy always said the twenty million gallons of water that spewed out of a North Carolina water main break was only half the amount that it would take to fill up the ego of Megan McCain.

My daddy always said it's very frightening when you wake up the commode with a heavy load then you flush and don't hear that water gush.

My daddy always said if you wake up with gravel in your gut and spit in your eye – don't`a blame`a him, he didn't`a make`a your pizza pie.

My daddy always said when doctors removed the two-hundred-pound wart from Hillary's ass all her worries were over when lab test revealed it was only Michelle Wolf clinging to her hope because Obama kept all the change.

My daddy always said the older you get is the older you get.

My daddy always said the best way to clear a room is with a big boisterous stanky beans and sardines fart.

My daddy always said if you smell a rat check your underwear before you check your wife's underwear.

My daddy always said some people look better dead.

My daddy always said – oh say did you see the fur flying at the demon – crats de - bait? Tulsi Gabbard didn't leave Kamala Harris enough fur to even make a camel toe thong.

My daddy always said he predicts that within the year 2020 some millennials will challenge the law and want to openly breast feed on their wife's or girlfriend's breast at the same time their baby is breast feeding. This will happen in an airport, or mall, or even at a Saints football game where the referees are all blind.

My daddy always said hunters and whores are just alike, they'll both do anything for a buck.

My daddy always said – when you have nothing – you have nothing to lose. When you have hemorrhoids – you have pain. When you have storms – you have rain. 'But' when you have Democrats - you have insane.

My daddy always said the Republicans worked hard, had two, three jobs. They saved money – built businesses – built homes and built careers. The Democrats built nothing – saved nothing and now they want a way, that's called a law, to get 'their unearned money out of your work-your-ass-off pockets.'

My daddy always said ladies, watch out for snakes when walking in the halls of Congress. They are all poisonous and will bite your money-maker without warning.

My daddy always said does your other half smell like a goat or fish? There is a cure for that, it's called soap and water. Does your grandma or grandpa smell like – – it? There's a cure for that, it's called soap and water. Does your crazy – creepy – V.P. - touchy – feely uncle Joe act like a sleaze ball and sniff you like a sleaze ball? There isn't a cure for that.

My daddy always said – Democrats are the reason we have warning labels on plastic fruit.

My daddy always said when people are running for public office the first time it's called a campaign. When reelection rolls around, it becomes a scam – paign.

My daddy always said the best way to keep our towns, cities, and states clean and litter free is term limits.

My daddy always said the first time he saw Nancy Pelosi, his first thought was my God that woman has been in bed with Al Sharpton's plastic surgeon.

My daddy always said Chuck U. Schumer said, "Mr. President, let's put your wall on a bus. If it gets off at Wall Street, you get the money. If it gets off at High Street, quit smoking crack."

My daddy always said while the two thieving nuns in Torrance, California stole over a half million dollars from the Catholic Church's 'catholic school,' they were filmed flipping the bird to all the Democrats that were left hungry and couldn't pass the third grade.

My daddy always said watch out Joe 'plugs' Biden! That senator, who identified as an Indian to get free college a.k.a. fake-a-hontas Warren, is on the warpath and she is out to scalp your plugs.

My daddy always said after my mother named her ass Christmas – every morning at breakfast he would sing that Christmas song, "I'll be home for Christmas."

My daddy always said when the president was asked if he believed mental illness runs in the congress and senate he said, "You betcha! Every election cycle they're running like crazy to get elected and prove to the American people that there is a house chocked full of nuts."

My daddy always said when Taylor Swift 'jumped ship' from the banana boat to the banana split, she still couldn't find anybody to spank her monkey.

My daddy always said weaker of the house, Nancy Pelosi, is adding to the rules of the house of representatives that all newly elected members must be potty trained. This new rule is retroactive to include Adam Schiff, Jerrold Nadler, and Elijah Cummings.

My daddy always said it doesn't make sense that businesses will spend millions of dollars advertising to get people into their stores but spend nothing on getting the customer checked out and on their way. If there are three registers – one cashier, six registers – one cashier, twelve registers – two cashiers, 'online' – no 'in line' wait time.

My daddy always said weaker of the house said July 4th will be her Independence Day. She will roll the stone away and celebrate never having to change another new house member's diaper.

My daddy always said he never understood why all the supposedly college educated weather readers and news readers can't pronounce the name of the land mass between Louisiana and Alabama.

My daddy always said everybody knows that Oregon is the beaver state and Missouri is the show me state. Does that mean everyone from Oregon visiting Missouri has to show their beaver?

My daddy always said you can always tell the difference between a pitcher and a pitcher. One scratches his ass, rubs his balls, the other rattles ice and pours cold drinks.

My daddy always said he knew the farmers had arrived at the right century when on the back of a hay truck a sign read my grass identifies as hay when cut and baled.

My daddy always said what did the pediatrician doctor say to the new nurse that was complaining about a waiting room full of snotty nose kids? "Nurse, you've heard of the money shot, right? Well what you see in that waiting room is the money snot."

My daddy always said did you fart, said the nose to the ass? The ass said no, it was just gas. Then the nose said to the ass, who do you think I am, a Democrat?

My daddy always said what do you have when you have Jerry Seinfeld, Jerry Lewis and Hillary Clinton in a car looking for a coffee shop? Two nuts and a sore loser.

My daddy always said Speaker of the House Nancy Pelosi was livid after the 2018 midterm election was over and the new members were sworn in. Not a single one was house broken and less than 10% were paper or litter box trained.

My daddy always said have you been exposed to 'ass – best – out?' If you have that feeling just below the heart and it moves down through the stomach until you have to fart, then that's a good case of ass-gas-best-out.

My daddy always said what is the number one state where you go on vacation and leave on probation? That would be the great state of Florida.

My daddy always said who's been flipping? Who's been flopping? Who – Joe – Joe, who – Joe bite me Biden? Who's been cowing? Who's been cowering – who – Joe – Joe who? Joe smell my hair – Joe smell my butt air – 'Joe smell defeat.' That's not smell the 'feet' Joe, that's smell 'defeat.' You can always grow a beak and peck 'it' with Hill – O - ry.

My daddy always said there is no future for those who live in the past.

My daddy always said what is the best chant the Democrats can start chanting? "Drop out Joe" – "Drop out Joe" – make room for the camel toe. "Drop out Joe" – "Drop out Joe" make room for Larry – Curly and Moe. "Drop out Joe" – "Drop out Joe" it's past time for you to go. "Drop out Joe" there's a fake Indian after your 'plugs."

My daddy always said the Democrats are having a November sale – buy one Democrat vote and get the rest for free.

My daddy always said he had a lot of people that loved him. They loved him when he got his old ass off 'their road' and out of 'their way.'

My daddy always said what did the cop say to the carload of teenagers he pulled over for speeding, found to be under the influence? "What we have here is teenage thinking."

My daddy always said when it came down to the nut cutting session in both houses of congress, none of the men had any balls. They all had to borrow a pair from Tulsi Gabbard.

My daddy always said don't worry about the teen dating app, the lesbian dating app, the singles or seniors dating apps because just launched today is 'dead as a doornail in a coffin' dating app. That's right… brain dead people will soon part with their money in order to date in the afterlife.

My daddy always said that slick Willie says the world doesn't know what a hellhole is until they try to have sex with Hilda beast, in or out of Bal-to-ti-I-more.

My daddy always said the only taste difference between Michelob Ultra-Light Beer and a public swimming pool full of grammar school kids is one has less chlorine.

My daddy always said space between the ears is 'educators lost frontier.' All the ones that slip through the cracks, end up on taxpayers backs as elected politicians or D.M.V. employees.

My daddy always said Elon Musk has bought launch and landing pads on Whoopi's ass, but he lost the bid on her forty-acre spread and mule.

My daddy always said when the audience of The View complained of a dead animal smell, dogs were brought in to sniff out the odor. It was soon determined that two of the host hadn't changed their diapers over the weekend.

My daddy always said yesterday, when I was dumb, I would put wet boggers on my tongue. Now that I'm older and smart, I dry my boggers with a fart.

My daddy always said the difference between a bat and a dingbat is one flies through the air and the other runs her fingers through your hair.

My daddy always said I know you have heard of this; you have heard of that. You have heard of nis; you have heard of nat. You have heard of loose; you have heard of goose, but does anyone believe fake-a-hontas slept in a papoose?

My daddy always said stand up for diarrhea! Don't sit on the throne for 'it'. Stand up, bend over and end zone 'it'. This is the Montezuma challenge.

My daddy always said Hillary's sun block won't keep her ass from burning in hell.

My daddy always said Kim Kardashian is going to study tax law because she wants to know if she can claim her left ass cheek and her right ass cheek as two dependents.

My daddy always said what's the one thing Taylor Swift can do that Hillary Clinton can't do? 'Draw a crowd without flies.'

My daddy always said what do liberals say when another gay or lesbian comes out of the closet? Different strokes, different pokes for different folks.

My daddy always said who amongst the Democratic presidential hopefuls said I'd walk a mile barefooted through broken glass just to smell the hair on Tulsi Gabbard's ass. 'Who?' You have twenty guesses but nineteen don't count. "Hey Joe, what chu got cooking?"

My daddy always said doctors in weird-ville have discovered the first case ever of 'nose lice.' Yes, you read that right, 'nose lice.' One of the presidential Democrat hopefuls has come down with a bad – bad case of nose lice brought on by the constant sniffing of hair, hello Joe.

My daddy always said when the reporter asked Tulsi Gabbard what her position is on the 'less meat' = 'less heat' proposal she replied, "You must be talking about Elizabeth Warren because I'm getting all the meat I can handle."

My daddy always said nobody's home to help the president deal with the rats and rodents. They all left Washington on a world tour of all the five-star hotels and private chef dinners. The good news is there's a bill before congress that would allow the citizens, both legal and illegal, of Elijah Cumming's district to claim both rats and rodents as dependents on their tax returns. "Butt" there is always a but somewhere. Boss rat said, "No soup for you President Trump – leave my rats alone!"

My daddy always said doctors have discovered a cure for hemorrhoids. Vote them out of office.

My daddy always said when you see those infomercials advertising dis – dat – do – poo – loose – goose and everything but the papoose and they say order now, operators are standing by, they are lying their asses off. What they should be saying is operators are laughing their asses off, if you call to order this crap.

My daddy always said Walter Reed's doctors have discovered why Speaker of the House Nancy Pelosi's face is contorted as if sitting on a toilet with a bad case of constipation. The speaker's ass was covered with ticks. You know, the usual suspects… the A's, the O's and the C's along with the rest of the wanna-B's.

My daddy always said what do you have if you have Nancy Pelosi, Jerry Nadler and Alexandria Ocasio Cortez in a hot tub together? Two beavers and a skunk.

My daddy always said when he married Lucie, he never dreamed the Navy's seventh fleet would all be docking in Port St. Lucie.

My daddy always said when Nancy Pelosi Speaker of the House held a news conference a reporter said, "Madam speaker, what have you learned being in front of the camera every day?" The speakers reply – "That there's no amount of make-up that can help me."

My daddy always said when Speaker of the House Nancy Pelosi called Alexandria Ocasio Cortez into her office for a private one-on-one session, did she spank her 'ass' or her 'monkey'? Fake news wants to know.

My daddy always said since Martha Stewart's Dogg ran away from home will she get a new puppy or cross the border and get herself a little kitty?

My daddy always said there is a rumor going around that there is a city near D.C. that's called rat town but the "mice troll" of the congressional district prefers for people to call it rodent sanctuary city. So if you come near – have no fear – because boss rat has the voting machine in 'high' gear.

My daddy always said what did Lorena Bobbitt say to her husband John Wayne Bobbitt after cutting off his penis? "It won't be long now!"

My daddy always said it's perfectly – fine – alright – very good of you "to love your neighbor." Just don't pull down her underwear while you're doing it.

"My momma always said, "Son, don't believe a damn word your daddy ever said."

The End

Now you can go eat your beans and sardines.

This book is meant to provoke you to toke before a poke, so you won't have to be parking horses or poking old fake-a-hontas. Now – now, so anyway – every day – just saying – if you can't read between the lines then get yourself a gallon of Hillary's mad-dog 20-20 wine. That wine and a toke - with a poke will get you woke - then you'll be reading what's left but believing only what's right. "Butt, there is always a butt." Your journey of reading will take you higher than any old toke. Besides, Katie Hill will soon be running for president and she will kick the 'fake Indian' under the bus and start brushing A.O.C.'s hair. The Republicans won't even notice, and the Democrats won't even care if Katie brushes or just parts hair. So put your tongues back in your mouth, Katie was just visiting down south. If you are not woke by now just stay asleep, nobody will miss you not even me.

-C. Birdfinger

www.ingramcontent.com/pod-product-compliance
Lightning Source LLC
LaVergne TN
LVHW051523070426
835507LV00023B/3267